Postcard C [barcode: C000246842]
— the fun

There's no doubt about it – postcard col fun. An absorbing, relaxing, escapist ho , that will also lead you into many new friendships, made through personal contacts at clubs or fairs, or through correspondence. There are tens of thousands of people throughout the world who enjoy collecting postcards!

The hobby is probably strongest and best-organised in Britain and France, where large fairs have been established for many years. North America has thousands of postcard devotees, but the longer distances involved make contact more difficult. In the United States, many clubs exist to cater for enthusiasts on a regional basis, and most organise their own shows. There, postcard collectors are called "deltiologists", but this rather cumbersome word has not found favour in Britain, where the title "cartologists" is sometimes used. Mostly, however, "postcard collectors" is the simplest way to describe those hooked on the hobby, which is now expanding and finding favour in most Western European countries, Australasia and South Africa.

Chromolithograph postcard: glamour and a good luck symbol (the mushroom).

Why is postcard collecting so popular?

Many people begin collecting picture postcards by accident, when an album originally put together by their grandparents or parents is handed down to them. They usually decide to either sell it or – if they are attracted by the cards – keep it and add to the collection. Others merely save the postcards sent to them by friends and relatives and build up a collection that way, until they decide to expand into a wider selection of contemporary cards, or even into old ones.

"ON THE KNEE."

A number of people start because they want to accumulate a collection of cards about a theme in which they're interested, or on the area in which they live.

To some collectors, postcards are about nostalgia, because they portray a different way of life in the town or village they live in. To others they're beautiful objects, even works of art. Then, of course, there are those who see postcards as a good investment – but more of that later.

Millar and Lang comic card from about 1905, illustrating a catch-phrase of the period.

1

New or old?

Thousands of people today probably collect postcards without ever realising that there exist millions of cards published before the Great War. Saving cards sent by friends on holidays, buying postcard souvenirs at museums, gift shops and at the seaside is a universal practice. But there was, in the early part of the century, a craze for buying, sending and collecting picture postcards that extended virtually worldwide ...

The period between 1900 and 1914 is generally referred to as the "Golden Age" of postcards, because this is the time they became established as the most widely-used method for personal communication. In the pre-telephone era, and before news pictures in the daily papers became commonplace, postcards served as the cheapest and most reliable method of sending messages, as an ideal medium for illustrating local and national events, and as a reflection of the age. It is no exaggeration to say that virtually every conceivable subject can be found depicted or satirised on picture postcards. Postcard publishers competed to produce designs to please the general public, and collecting postcards became a national pastime, at least among the middle and upper classes, where most families would save the cards they received and mount them in albums. When re-discovered today, Edwardian albums can reflect the life-style of the family that owned them: those with rich friends or relatives could

Landing the cockles at Leigh-on-Sea, probably in the 1920's. This type of 'Social History' card is very popular.

boast of cards illustrating European tours: others, more modestly show off Blackpool or Skegness.

In the first decade of the century, hobby magazines promoted postcard collecting, and cards were poured out to cater for what became a craze. Truly, in pre-1914 postcards, *"all human life was there"*.

The Great War actually stimulated postcard production, with a wave of patriotic and sentimental cards, but it destroyed a national mood.

From 1918, all kinds of things combined to bring about a virtual extinction of postcard collecting as a hobby; only scenic views, Art Deco, and comic postcards dragged it through to the 1950's. The doubling of the inland postage rate for postcards from a halfpenny to a penny, the increased use of the telephone (encouraged, ironically, by slogans that can be found on the backs of postcards), more expensive paper, more efficient and interesting newspapers, and a radically altered set of social attitudes were all contributory factors.

Cards of the "Golden Age" lay dormant, unloved and largely unseen, until a small group of collectors in the 1950's began to re-awaken interest in them. The revival of

'Language of Flowers' postcard, published by Felix Rosenstiel. Several series on this theme can be found.

Embossed pig design from a marvellous series published by Misch & Stock titled the "Millionaire". Cards like this would cost about £6.

postcard collecting as a hobby did not accelerate until the early 1970's, partly stimulated by a travelling exhibition put on by the Victoria and Albert Museum, though several years before this, a postcard magazine had been started, and a national postcard club set up.

It is possible to argue that collectors of 'old' and 'modern' cards are two separate types, but in reality there is a considerable overlap, and most enthusiasts would welcome chances to add to their collections by obtaining cards of any era. The relative lack of material from the 1918-50 period does mean that it is *possible* to put your postcard collecting into one time compartment or other, but this is becoming less common.

However, there are still distinct differences in the way older – compared with more recent – postcards are described, priced and collected. The major part of this book deals with older cards, those that have traditionally been popular since the collecting revival a couple of decades ago. Modern cards are discussed from page 23 onwards.

Collectors should always go for the postcards they like, regardless of antiquity or modernity.

Cards to suit every pocket

There exists among nonpostcard collectors the myth that old cards must be worth money, simply because they are old. But prices of objects that are in themselves of no value are governed by how many collectors want them, and how many of the objects there are. Popular cards need

Edwardian actresses used postcards as publicity handouts, and today cards like this exist in vast quantities, selling at around 30p. The featured lady here is Miss Sybil Arundale; she's on a card published by the Rotophoto Co.

Raphael Tuck 'In the Air' series 1. The aviation era that began in the first decade of the century spanned a whole range of aviation cards, including meetings, personalities and planes.

not necessarily be expensive ones. Prices can be influenced by catalogues and auctions, but a reasonable price for any postcard is in the end established by the demand for it.

Demand for postcards is largely governed by the subject matter of the picture. An eighty-year old view of Lake Windermere that looks pretty much the same in 1989 as in 1905 is worth no more than a couple of pence, unless it's a scarce card by a sought-after or obscure publisher. Deckleedged greetings cards of the 1920's or 1930's can now be bought for next to nothing. Views of Cathedrals, with exceptions, are valued in pence. All these types are cheap because most people consider them unattractive or common (and therefore undesirable), but this is no reason to forego collecting them. It is often cheapest to establish collecting fashions yourself!

Making blanket statements about popular or unpopular cards is, of course, only 90% of the truth. All three categories quoted above have their desirable exceptions: the hold-to-light cathedral, the railway 'official' that looks on the surface like a common viewcard, the greetings card that includes a popular motif or theme. But generally, they're among the 'also-rans' in collectors' demands.

It still pays to be an expert and learn about whatever branch of the hobby you choose, though. A church exterior might look worthless to one collector; but that postcard might be a rare item to a topographical collector who has never seen it.

Animated street scene at Baildon, Yorkshire, by anonymous publisher.

Common views of towns and cities should be worth only a few pence.

Scenic views, even old ones, are not very collectable. This is a card of the old mill at Jesmond Dene.

A photographic card of a church at Southery, Norfolk, posted from the village in July 1909.

What, then, does define popular postcards?

In the days before 1914, the 'first era' of picture postcard collecting, many people's tastes were random – they kept the cards they were sent, often in no particular order (other than date of receipt). Some collectors amassed albums of Churches, German views, beautiful girls and so on. Nowadays, the majority of postcard collectors specialise in one of the following ways:

(1) **By area.** Collectors who seek cards of a particular village, town, city or county are known as 'topographical' collectors. 'Topographicals' are viewcards, whether of countryside or built-up areas. This was a style of collecting less popular with our Edwardian predecessors, for their viewcards then were of con-temporary and familiar scenes. National publishers in the 1900-14 period concentrated their topographical output on city centres and tourist loca-tions, and certainly did not in-vest them with the same status as their subject and artistic postcard issues.

Topographical collecting had a low priority then, and so it did at the rebirth of the hob-by in the 1950's. Indeed, not until the late 1970's did this style of postcard collecting become really fashionable. Now, the sought-after cards are real photographs of villages and suburban streets, largely by local photographers who produced only small quan-tities, sometimes in anonymity. As a generation of 'topo' col-lectors has grown in ex-perience, so the relative scarci-ty of material has begun to be appreciated. Good animated street scenes are now edging into double figures as a norm. Because of this, fears have been expressed that escalating prices will deter new collectors from taking on a 'topo' ambi-tion. Yet there remains a vast quantity of cheaper viewcards and street scenes, and the cur-rent increase in prices merely reflects the situation of supply and demand. Even the most expensive postcards are cheaper than cigarette cards or stamps of a similar status.

In any case, the fashion for 'topos' may well subside as de-mand for other types becomes stronger.

Topographical collecting is based on nostalgia, and on historical and social interest. In this latter category, there is an overlap with subject collecting. Cards from overseas (outside G.B.) have increased enor-mously in popularity in the last three years, with a following for virtually any country.

Especially popular are British Commonwealth and South American or African material.

(2) **By subject or theme.** What a postcard collector appreciates is often determined by his or her other interests. Sport, a job, or another hobby might influence the selection of a theme. Railway stations, lifeboats, road transport, coalmines, windmills, shops and delivery vehicles on postcards are all highly popular subjects, and all these cards are probably being sought by 'topo' collectors as well – hence these types too have moved rapidly upwards in price in the last couple of years.

Subjects or themes, though, can span any price bracket, and include both serious and comic cards. Trying to collect postcards showing interiors of village railway stations with trains pulling in and porters carrying baggage would now be quite an expensive proposition – but have a look for cards featuring umbrellas, elephants or clocks (not all on the same card!) and you might find your pound goes a little further. Many people have gone imaginatively for more unusual themes and built up fascinating collections.

Currently in vogue are sport postcards – particularly cricket, football, golf and tennis – and indoor games such as billiards, chess or table tennis. Transport themes are popular (railways, road transport, shipping and aviation all have strong followings), and royalty is a perennial favourite. Military postcards, both photographic and artist-drawn, are always in demand, and Animals (especially cats, dogs, horses and pigs) much-appreciated.

Cynicus was the pseudonym of Scottish artist Martin Anderson, who both drew and published many fine satirical comic cards.

Harry Payne is recognised as the finest military artist who drew for postcards. This is in a series called 'Regimental Badges & Their Wearers' published by Raphael Tuck.

It's always a useful idea, though, to develop a category of your own and build it up, as an 'extra' to any other types of card you might collect.

(3) **By artist.** Picture postcards are a miniature art form, and an extremely cheap way of building up your own art gallery. You can find the works of most famous pre-twentieth century artists reproduced on postcards, usually costing around 30 pence a card. Much more popular, appreciated and valued in the postcard world are those artists who either designed specifically or principally for the picture postcard, or worked contemporaneously with the "Golden Age". Edwardian publishers including Raphael Tuck, Hildesheimer and Davidson Bros. commissioned work especially for their postcard productions.

The choice is wide: landscape artists, cartoonists, artists in a particular style. There are hundreds to choose from, and many have had their cards well-listed and catalogued. Again, you can spend a fortune or a song. Most landscape artists' cards are freely available, and even those of the currently most popular, A.R. Quinton, range from only 50p-£1.50. At the moment it is relatively easy and inexpensive to amass a collection of postcards of any one of a number of such artists, with 30p a card a sensible norm.

Comic cards by named artists are more expensive, largely because these were fashionable to collect in the 1960's and the early postcard catalogues reflected their then popularity.

It is arguable that many are now overpriced, including

5

those of Tom Browne, whose cards are freely available yet average more than £2 each in dealers' stocks, Phil May, Dudley Hardy and John Hassall. Demand for the last three is currently lukewarm, yet prices still hover around £4 a card.

Names less in vogue among collectors of twenty years ago – Donald McGill, Cynicus (Martin Anderson), G.E. Shepheard, and Lawson Wood – generally retail at more realistic levels.

The most popular postcard artist of all is Louis Wain, who drew serio-comic pictures of cats and had hundreds of postcard designs published. Another vogue artist of the sixties, the price of his cards increased too quickly and suffered collector resistance. His work is now again much sought-after, and good condition examples command prices in excess of £10.

Artists whose work has increased markedly in price in the 1980's include R.P. Phillimore, a landscape/historical artist who published his own highly attractive and individual cards, and G.E. Studdy, creator of the famous 'Bonzo' dog. In both cases, though, the prices may well run out of steam if new collectors don't come along to mop up the commoner material. It is an unfortunate fact that a majority of postcard dealers do not discriminate between common and scarce material for an artist who is quoted at a fixed price in a postcard catalogue. This, as much as anything, is likely to deter new collectors from starting on the work of some of the artists mentioned here.

If you really want to spend money, then Art Nouveau ar-

One of Raphael Kirchner's "Enfants de la Mer" set of 12. Each card in this series is likely to cost about £25.

Donald McGill was undoubtedly the king of postcard artists, producing thousands of designs over a sixty-year period. This is a typical example from the 1930's published by Woolstone Bros.

tists, of whom Alphonse Mucha and Raphael Kirchner are the most collected, is the area to go for. Really scarce Muchas have broken the hundred-pound barrier. Even scarcer are cards by Toulouse-Lautrec, where you can quadruple that latter figure.

(4) **By publisher.** Stamps are categorised according to country of origin, postcards by their publisher. Most collectors, though, do not worry too much about this, and their collections transcend publisher boundaries. It's an area for keen researchers, for building checklists, an area more akin to purist stamp collecting than 'topo' or 'subject' collecting.

National publishers were helpful – they usually issued postcards in sets of six, and printed series numbers and titles clearly on the back. Local publishers were not always so co-operative, sometimes resorting to handwritten numbers and captions, or even none at all.

Of the national British publishers, the cards of Raphael Tuck have been best catalogued and most frequently written about. Tuck collectors are actually more prolific in the United States – the firm also produced issues specially for the U.S. – than in their home country. One fascinating project would be to build up a collection including an example of each style of Tuck card published – and it wouldn't be too expensive, either.

Bamforth's of Holmfirth, famous for their comic and song/hymn postcards, have also been extensively researched. Both is firm and Tuck have had catalogues published that are devoted specifically to their cards – interestingly, both books emanate from the U.S.A.

Louis Levy, a French-originating publisher around whose work there is a good deal of mystery, produced prolifically in France and Britain, and has an excellent collector following in both countries.

Plenty of research, too, has been done on some 'area' publishers who operated over a range of counties – F.G.O. Stuart of Southampton, J. Welch of Portsmouth, and the Abraham brothers of Keswick spring to mind – and extensive and admirable studies on local publishers concentrating on one town and its surrounding villages have been undertaken.

Collecting by publisher has much to recommend it. Putting together a representative selection of most national firms would be quite cheap, and would provide an interesting variety of cards. Good examples to go for might be Valentine's of Dundee, Rotary Photo Co., or Wrench.

(5) **By style or type.** Postcards come in all shapes, sizes, types and materials. Many are classed as novelties – cards of strange size, with a part cut out to achieve a 'moonlight' effect, or unorthodox material.

'Pull-outs' that reveal a dozen views of a particular location, or 'cut-outs' that make a model. Novelty cards are not popular as a genre, though certain types command quite high prices. Catalogue values of these cards are normally too high.

One popular collecting field is in 'silk' postcards. Most originate from the First World War, when embroidered silks with sentimental messages were bought by allied troops.

Lovely shipping (Carron Line) advertising card – would sell for about £20.

One of a beautiful chromo set of twelve published by C.W. Faulkner, and posted on Guernsey in October 1905.

C.H. Twelvetrees specialised in comic situations involving children. Card by the Alpha Publishing Co. of London, postmarked October 1917.

Because they were treasured, a huge number have survived and are consequently less expensive than most people suppose. The best embroidered silk cards are those featuring regimental crests or town names.

Much more highly-rated are woven silks, mostly published pre-1914. Favourite designs here are of ships.

Plenty of cheap cards fall into a 'type' collecting

Real photographic cards of railway stations are highly-sought after. This is Kelmscot and Langford in Oxfordshire.

Bamforths of Holmfirth published many hundreds of song cards and hymn cards in sets of three or four. Many featured first world war sentiment.

category — possibilities are silhouettes, moonlights, or large letters/year dates.

It would be pleasant to say that some people collect by **'messages'**, but despite an enormous interest in what was written on the reverse of the card, it would perhaps be an exaggeration to say that anyone specifically *collected* this way. Original Edwardian albums often tell a fascinating family story, and individual cards can reveal intriguing correspondence or the signature of a famous person. The best messages can be on the cheapest cards, too! It's common to hear non-postcard collectors say *"the other side's the most interesting"* and ignore the picture. Dealers don't yet have special classifications for 'interesting messages', though. You have to find them yourself!

One collector is aiming to acquire a card collection featuring a postmark of each date this century. Now that's an intriguing thought!

Open-ended collecting

Postcards, unlike stamps or cigarette cards, are not exhaustively catalogued. British stamp issues, including varieties, are listed from the start in 1840, but it's not possible — yet — to do the same thing with postcards. Certain artists and subjects have been well-documented, and definitive checklists have been published in book form for the postcards of Tom Browne, Lance Thackeray, Alphonse Mucha, Philip Boileau and Harry Payne, for the publishers Bamforth, and for railway 'official' and silk cards. The publishers Tuck have been part-documented, and there are lots of checklists in private circulation. But the new collector in the vast majority of postcard categories will find no reference list to help. That's partly what makes postcards such fun. It's an open-ended search: you don't always know what you're looking for, and you're never quite sure what you'll find next! It's likely that during the next few years, many more areas will be documented. Perhaps in twenty years the situation will have dramatically changed, with computerised checklists available for all categories. At the moment, it is comparitively easy for someone to become an expert in a particular field quite quickly.

Starting a collection

Most postcard collectors do eventually specialise in one or several areas of the hobby. But if you're not quite sure what type to collect it's a good idea to keep an open mind, and read about, and look at, as many sorts of postcards as you can.

The best rule early on is *buy the cards you like.* That way at least you'll enjoy your early collection. There's no need to be too ambitious about price, or buy expensive cards, while you're still learning. But it is important to become familiar with pricing structures as quickly as you can, so that you know what is a reasonable price for a card you want. Learning about all types of postcards and keeping in touch with the postcard scene is important, too. It is fashionable in some collecting fields to ignore printed works on the hobby in question; but building up your knowledge about picture postcards will not only make the collecting of them more enjoyable, it will probably have financial advantages as well. *Picture Postcard Monthly* keeps collectors in touch with trends and developments of the hobby and provides research and background reading. There are three British postcard catalogues to choose from as guides to prices.

Where to buy

The postcard collector of 1989 is provided with an embarrassment of riches in terms of sources of material compared with his or her counterpart of the 1950's/60's. Junk and antique shops were then a prime source, and the 'penny black and white, twopence coloured' principle obtained for a long time. Publicity stimulated by the collecting revival actually had the result of bringing many more postcards onto the market, and specialist dealers began to buy original collections and sell a large proportion via postal lists. A few fairs were organised with the aim of attracting collectors to an event where they had access to a selection of dealers. In 1976, the 'British International Postcard Exhibition' was the first of what has been ever since an annual showpiece.

Now there are regular *specialist postcard* fairs, as well as many general collectors' fairs that include cards. Around 300 specialist dealers cater for the hobby, and many operate an approval service. You can find out what's on in your area by checking adverts in your local press, or by consulting the Diary in *Picture Postcard Monthly.*

Another source of cards is at auction.

Card Condition

Wherever you buy you should be careful to buy cards in the best available condition. **Experience will tell you which cards are common and which rare, but in most cases it's worth waiting for a better example of the same or a similar card. This is especially true at fairs, where you might have a choice of up to a hundred dealers. Catalogue prices relate to cards in top condition. Creased, torn, scuffed or otherwise damaged cards should be downgraded in price, often drastically.**

Try to ignore such cards anyway, unless you are desperate to acquire a particular scarce item. Other postcards to avoid are ones that are foxed (with ugly brown stains – most prevalent on silk cards), or water-damaged. This latter condition leads to parting of the pieces of card that make up the finished postcard, and can be recognised by a 'soft' or 'thinned' feel to part of the card. Bundles of cards exposed to very damp conditions can exhibit this feature, and should be strenuously ignored.

Faded photographic cards are not items to go for, either, and it is not pleasing to see fronts (picture-sides) of

Landscapes by Henry Wimbush can make a charming collection. This is a scene of Ullswater from 'Picturesque English Lakes' (Raphael Tuck). 40p is around the right figure for what are very common cards.

This design is known as a 'fantasy head': the skull design is made up of a pair of lovers, and wine-glasses on a table. Not as popular as a few years ago, a card like this would cost about £10.

postcards defaced by pen marks. Early (pre-1902) postcards with undivided backs actually had a space for writing a message, and provided such writing does not obscure or overshadow the picture, it can actually complement the card.

Look out for damage on the back, too – cards that were once *stuck* in albums often have ugly reverse markings, and sometimes the back can have been defaced by a dealer's handstamp. The most famous of these is the 'Hogsthorpe Horror' or Skegness Postcard Library. How much such handstamps detract from the overall attractiveness of the card is debatable, but some collectors do avoid cards with this problem.

Cards with stamps removed *may* be acceptable, provided the front (picture side) has not been damaged.

Postcards depend to a large extent on visual attractiveness for their appeal, and items in the finest condition will also look best in an album – and be most readily re-saleable. Defects are not always apparent on first glance, especially where the lighting at a fair leaves something to be desired. Many helpful dealers write 'w.a.f.' (with all faults) next to the price, but don't usually specify what the fault is. *Always make sure the price reflects the condition of the card.*

Auction lot descriptions should always include remarks about the state of the cards.

Two other categories of cards to avoid for reasons other than condition: modern reproductions of old cards (unless they're the *modern price*) and postcards that are just too expensive. The customer always has the ultimate sanction: refuse to pay for a card that you feel is too inflated in price.

Postcard collectors are not as fussy about condition as their counterparts in stamps and cigarette cards – but the trend towards demanding top quality material is noticeable, and will continue.

How to win at fairs

A postcard fair is an exciting experience. For about six hours you can escape from the world and enjoy friendly company in safe, warm surroundings. Often the refreshments are good, too! The tremendous thing about these specialist fairs is the amount of material on view. It's simply staggering. The biggest regular is held at the 'Royal National' Hotel, Woburn Place, London (nearest tube station: Russell Square) every month, when about 120 tables full of postcards are on view. It's generally referred to as the 'Bloomsbury', after the area in which the hotel is located.

You could spend a week there looking for cards and still miss half of what was on offer! Faced with such an array of goodies, you must be systematic. That means using your table plan (list of dealers on numbered tables, given out at most specialist events) to pinpoint exactly where you've been and what you've looked for.

If you're a beginner you could have a smashing time just wandering round looking at what was available. In this way you could learn a tremendous amount about the hobby in one day. If you know what you're looking for, it's still advisable to have a plan of campaign: to tour the room in a certain direction, asking dealers specifically for the type of cards you require. Some collectors make more than one tour: on their first trip they'll look for the collecting interest where they know the cards are hardest to find; on the second time around they'll search for other avenues of collecting in a more relaxed fashion. 'Old hands' at the fairs know the dealers who specialise in a certain type of card – foreign, comic, topographical, glamour – and who might therefore have useful relevant material.

Pacing yourself at a fair is crucial! Six hours of postcard searching can be extremely tiring: breaks for refreshment, preferably away from what is often quite a hurly-burly, are recommended, and a ten-minute stay at a stall where there are chairs provided can do wonders for flagging morale.

Dealers are by and large friendly and helpful, and most collectors strike up a good relationship with them. Fairs can be quite good social events, too! Dealers do, however, like customers to handle their cards carefully, and to put unwanted cards back in the same place they came from. Some file their postcards behind, others in front of, subject headings: it's easy to find out which and keep those cards in the correct spot.

Once you've got a growing collection of a particular place, artist, publisher, or subject (or indeed a number of growing collections!) it's advisable to take a checklist with you – either a written one or in the form of photocopies – to avoid buying duplicate cards.

British Social History: Whitchurch cheese fair, with a fine selection on view.

Cornish beach by Jotter (Hayward Young), published by Tuck

Australian cricket tourists 1905 on a card published by Hartmann of London. It features the players' photographs, and a list of test venues and dates.

Seaside/bathing comics are many people's idea of what a picture postcard is all about. They haven't caught on too well with collectors, though, and can be picked up very cheaply.

Hop-picking scenes are much sought-after by collectors, though this series by Young & Cooper of Maidstone is the commonest of the Kent cards.

Trams at Southsea Common provide an extremely common postcard view, which ought to retail at 50p or so.

One of the engaging designs of Tom Browne, whose sketches of Edwardian life appear on hundreds of postcards. Expect to pay £2 each for them, though.

Embossed 'shrimp border' design with view of Talbot Square, Blackpool, inside. Boots postcard in the 'Pelham' series, posted at Blackpool in August 1907.

Be prepared, too, by knowing the going prices for cards in the category you collect.

You can sell cards at fairs, too, but if you sell to a dealer who is going to resell the material, he will only offer a percentage (half to two-thirds) of his selling price.

Other specialist fairs are smaller than the 'Bloomsbury', but the same principles apply. Provincial events especially recommended are at Altrincham (Cresta Court Hotel), Brighton (Madeira Hotel), Cheltenham (Racecourse), Leeds (Pudsey Civic Hall), Chester (Freemasons Hall), and Nottingham (Lakeside Pavilion, University).

General collectors' fairs can be rewarding if a reasonable number of postcard dealers are present. It's best to check first with the organisers if you're travelling any distance. Antique fairs may reveal a few cards, but there's a much greater element of hit and miss with the pricing at · such events. Dealers who do not know much about cards but have heard they're worth money (!) usually err on the side of their advantage when pricing cards. It helps to be a postcard expert to spot the bargains, and such non-specialist fairs are definitely not recommended for the beginner.

Getting a good deal from approvals

Many dealers are prepared to send cards through the post to customers who've specified particular types they'd like. An approval service works well provided both parties work the system sensibly. Dealers who send regular, reasonably priced selections of relevant material not seen before by the collec-

The First World War soon encouraged British (and in this case, American) publishers to produce cards making fun of the Kaiser.

Fine postcard advertising Carl Hagenbeck's zoo and circus at Olympia.

tor will soon acquire a good reputation. Customers should pay promptly for material sent, and make sure returned cards are well-wrapped.

Collectors feel rightly aggrieved if they receive no reaction from dealers who've advertised an approval service after they've sent a wants list and S.A.E.

Customers, by the way, should expect to pay postage both ways unless they spend above a specified sum. Sending approvals is a time-consuming activity for dealers, and collectors are advised to be as specific as possible in their requests.

A general way of soliciting approvals is via a classified advert in PPM.

Buying at auction

It has become apparent in the last few years that many quality cards are now disappearing into auctions, where higher prices are expected. Prices have been obtained at auction for all sorts of postcards that wouldn't sell at fairs for anything like the same amount. All kinds of reasons have been advanced – different clientele, different psychology, focus on one card – but nobody has yet satisfactorily explained the phenomenon.

Auction realisations can be lower as well as higher, though. A high proportion of the larger lots at auction are bought by dealers, so it's a fair assumption that the vendor would have got a better price for that material had he sold direct – if, of course, he'd known where to go. But it's precisely the price uncertainty that makes auctions exciting.

One of the most desirable of all postcard types, a woven silk. This is a French-published card featuring Lord Kitchener, and would cost about £40.

Some of the most beautiful postcards were produced as birthday or seasonal greetings. This marvellous embossed example featuring children, doll, and Christmas tree would surely earn a place in anyone's collection.

Postcard auctions, like specialist fairs, have proliferated in the past few years. The standard of lot description and cataloguing has improved, though it still varies enormously. Most British auctions offer bulk lots, but the trend towards concentrating on single cards – as is typical of German and United States auctions, where most lots are illustrated – is gaining momentum. This trend, of course, favours the collector rather than the dealer.

First in the field with a Specialised Postcard Auction was Ken Lawson, whose firm – of that name – established a standard for others to emulate.

If you buy cards from auction, then personal viewing is highly recommended unless the items are singles, well-described and illustrated. Multi-card lots should always be checked very carefully for condition and assessed correspondingly.

Personal attendance at the auction itself isn't so necessary – though it's very interesting. It's always possible to leave or post a bid – the most you want to pay for a lot. If you're in the room and want to be cold and clinical about your purchases, decide on a limit for any lot and stick to it!

Postal bidders will have to pay postage and packing charges on top of their successful bid. Many auctions also add 10% (+ V.A.T.) buyers' commission to the 'hammer' price. Check the auction conditions carefully!

You can learn an awful lot at auctions though, by listening to the bids, seeing which material is in demand, assessing the competition for particular lots. A close study of the prices realised list in conjunction with the original catalogue is an extremely worthwhile exercise, too.

Buying privately

Once upon a time, a 'postcards wanted' advert in a local newspaper would flush out any number of old collections. Those days have basically gone. Tremendous publicity about the interest in old postcards at local and national level has brought shoals of albums out of attics. There are no doubt more waiting to be discovered: but those that now emerge are just as likely to go to a local auction to be sold.

If you *are* lucky enough to be offered an original family album, do consider keeping it intact: so many collections that told a story have been broken up and re-assembled into a multitude of thematic and topographical collections.

Postcard shops

There are now quite a lot of retail outlets which hold substantial stocks of postcards. The reference section of *Picture Postcard Annual* lists a number of specialised card or general collectors' shops – do support such shops if you're visiting an area where there is one.

Antique and bric-a-brac shops were at one time a useful source of old cards. Today you'll be lucky to find anything worthwhile: it only needs one knowledgeable dealer or collector to stumble on an untapped stock of reasonable material and the whole lot will probably be bought. Still, you can always hope you're the first to see them …

(continued on page 16)

Turn-of-the-century 'Gruss Aus (Greetings From) postcard. These are most commonly found from German and Austrian towns and tourist locations, and those from other countries can be quite rare. Features of the Gruss Aus style are the use of vignette pictures (usually four or five) and the beautiful printing styles.

Picture Postcards were r Post Office until 1894, altl use on the continent of Eurc British cards were known a mm), smaller than the con and the message had to be the picture, leaving the bac This obviously inhibited the so when the Post Office pe size card (1899) and the message and address oc publishers were able to exp effectively, and a flood of c ject was produced.

This booklet does not s history of the picture pos documented in other 'Bibliography').

Details of specialist and collectors' fairs where you can buy and sell postcards are published in *Picture Postcard Monthly* (see advert on back cover).

Court-size card from Douglas, Isle of Man, published by S.H. Broadbent & Co. Surprisingly, cards like this are not all that popular with collectors at the moment, though examples of British coloured cards in good condition are not easy to find. Postally used cards, especially from the place illustrated, and in conjunction with a Victorian stamp, are most desirable.

ically approved by the
they were in common
m the 1870's. The early
rt cards (size 115 x 89
l size of 140 x 89 mm,
en on the same side as
the stamp and address.
bilities for illustrations,
d the use of the larger-
d back' (1902) where
the same side, the
e postcard much more
n every imaginable sub-

to provide a detailed
which has been well-
irable works (see

NB The cards on this centrefold are shown actual size. In order to provide more illustrations, all the other postcards on pages 1-24 have been reduced from their actual size of 140 x 89 mm (or, in the case of the modern cards from 150 x 100 mm).

Modern postcards can be found at high street shops, but for limited edition or more unusual issues you have to visit premises specialising in moderns, or ask for sales lists from specialist dealers.

Discounts

Approval selections may come with the enticement of a percentage reduction if you buy a certain amount. Similarly, some dealers at fairs may reduce the total price of your purchases if they feel your package spending warrants it. If you feel an item at a fair is overpriced, you are quite justified in asking whether the dealer will take a reduced figure. But don't ask just for the sake of it – a dealer who's fixed a fair or even bargain price for a single item will not feel happy about being asked for discount on that.

Used or unused?

In most cases it does not particularly matter whether a card has been postally used or unused; the condition of the postcard is a more important factor. Some collectors prefer unused material in fine condition; others believe that a date of postal usage authenticates a card and makes it unique. Certainly a card with a related picture, postmark, and/or message is a little bit more special than an unused example. After all, the purpose of a postcard is to send a message through the postal system. Special postmarks can in fact add to the value of a card, especially in the Aviation field.

Particularly interesting are railway T.P.O.'s (travelling post offices) and similar, some exhibition postmarks, temporary skeleton and rubber postmarks and maritime and military cancellations.

Published by Sandle brothers, this attractive London card was posted in December 1899 to Osnabruck (see back, below).

Housing your collection

The quickest and convenient methods of housing postcards are in albums or boxes. The Edwardians used albums with ready-cut slots to slide the postcards into (as a result, many cards from these have noticeable triangular *album marks* in each corner). Nowadays, some collectors use these, but there are also many types of two, three, four, or six-to-page albums with plastic leaves for collectors to choose from. Some concern has been expressed about the possible long-term effects of keeping postcards in plastic albums, and most are now advertised as using acid-free plastic. Special boxes to keep cards can be bought each holding 400-500 items; a variety of paper/plastic envelopes is available so that each postcard can have its individual protector; the sections can then be separated by divider cards.

Neither of these methods is ideally designed for a collection to be written-up, though white card can be used in album pockets adjoining postcards, or inserted into the same envelope as a postcard in boxes. A less restrictive method is to make your own album out of a ring file binder and cardboard sheets. The postcards can then be arranged on a page in any formation and attached by album corners. A write-up can be included, and interleaving used for protection if necessary.

All three methods allow for some flexibility in placing new purchases into a numerical or alphabetical list, though in this respect the box is obviously most efficient.

Wallets with plastic pages holding about twenty cards are available, and can be useful for taking to fairs to display types of postcards needed. Another available aid is the postcard case, holding about 2,000 cards, and widely used by dealers.

Keeping a check

Many collectors face the problem of keeping a checklist up to date. Written lists in notebooks frequently need updating and soon become difficult to manage, but a list is usually necessary to avoid buying duplicate cards. An index system is easier to update, and some have even put research/checklists onto computer. If the collection is reasonably small or specialised, or the cards have no adequate caption or numbering system,

Poster advertising of products converted to the postcard medium very suitable. Cards like this are very popular and collectable – and would cost around £20.

One of the extremely long heraldic series published by Stoddart under the 'Ja-Ja' label.

then photocopies may prove useful as a reference.

Clubs: extending your contacts

Although a number of collectors prefer, or are forced by circumstances to pursue their hobby in isolation, most would find it beneficial to join a postcard club to make new contacts and friends. Clubs provide another source of material in that some time is usually spent in buying, selling or exchanging postcards. Talks, quizzes, and conversation will all help to broaden your knowledge and experience of the hobby. There may not in fact be a postcard club near you at the moment but the number is growing, and hopefully most areas of the country will be well catered-for within a few years.

Investment?

Try not to think about it. Postcards have so far largely escaped the attention of speculators, and hopefully will continue to do so. Collectors are pleased when they see the value of their cards increase, but conversely are worried when prices of items they wish to buy escalate. Price rises are a two-edged sword, though their worst feature is in possible deterrence of new collectors in a particular area.

The best way to look at your postcard collection is that its main purpose is to provide you with pleasure and enjoyment. If the cards appreciate in value as well, that is a bonus. It can be fun trying to guess which cards may rise in price next, but this should be a secondary motive to buying the postcards you like.

Looking back now at the first IPM postcard catalogue published in 1975, the prices are fascinating. Some cards that are now expensive were then rated very low, other 1975 high-flyers are not now so popular. Fashions in postcard collecting have changed. Had you spent money on certain types of card ten years ago you would have seen your holding rise in value many times. It's often said that if you'd known what to buy, you could have made a fortune! But, equally, there are plenty of cards that were not highly-rated in 1975 that have moved very little.

Remember, that to keep pace with inflation, a card would have had to increase in value by about 160% over the last fourteen years; a smaller increase than this, and the card is worth less in real terms.

By this standard, the following would not have proved good investments in 1975:

Suzanne Meunier glamour cards (£5 catalogue value in 1975, £8 now)
Boxer Rebellion cartoons (£8 in 1975, £12 now)
Embossed coin cards (£2.50 in 1975, £6 now)
Meteor transparencies (£8 in 1975, £10 now)

On the other hand, certain other categories have increased in value spectacularly:

Harrison Fisher glamour studies (60p in 1975, £4 now)
Animated Real Photo street scenes (30p in 1975, £12 now)
Early Louis Wains (£5 in 1975, £18 now)
Woven silk liners (£15 in 1975, £45 now)
Fred Spurgin comics (20p in 1975, £2 now)
Windmills (40p in 1975, £12 now)
Cinemas (£1 in 1975, £15 now)
Tin mining (40p in 1975, £15 now)

The rate of increase has not been uniform over the years, however. Greatest catalogue

Posted at Ealing in December 1907, this London street scene published by Louis Levy (LL) is full of interest. LL produced a huge series covering London (this is no. 169, New Bond Street) as well as hundreds of other towns and areas in England. Their cards covered France comprehensively.

Trams have always been among collectors' favourite subjects. This example from Mapperley, Nottingham, is even better for being published in the sought-after 'Clumber' series. It was posted at Nottingham in August 1908.

The French were really good at portraying crafts, occupations and real life in general. Not surprisingly, these cards can be highly elusive and rather expensive, because the demand for them from topographical collectors is huge.

movement across the board occurred in 1975/6, 1979, and 1987/8.

The moral is: collect what you like, and let the search, the collecting, the looking, and the writing-up give you pleasure.

In the end, if you have an interesting collection made up of cards in good condition, that collection will appeal to others.

Forget the investment. It's too much to worry about. On past performance, your purchases will probably reward you quite well, anyway.

Where and how to sell

Postcard collectors often want to sell parts of collections they have built up – because they've tired of a particular type, or want to release some cash to finance the purchase of more expensive cards. Sometimes, a complete collection might be offered for sale.

Either way, there are a number of methods of selling cards.

Remember that the price quoted in catalogues is the expected dealer's selling price. To sell your spare cards, or your collection, at that price you generally have to become a **temporary dealer** yourself. That means taking a table at a fair (with its attendant travelling and rental expenses) or producing a **sales list** (with postage and advertising costs). Either way the overheads will cut sizeably into your realisation. Nevertheless, that's how many collectors do become part-time dealers.

Getting the best price means going directly to the person(s) who might want your material. That's why a lot of vendors put their material into **auction.** This time their expenses are in the shape of the auction house's commission. This method does not guarantee a high price for your cards, for many lots at auction are bought by dealers aiming to resell at a profit. What is likely to happen is that your most desirable cards – choice single items – are likely to reach a

Meteor transparency – the lighthouse beam shines when held to the light. Cards like this have hardly changed in value since the mid-1970's.

Royalty is an extremely popular subject. Favourites are visits and Russian royals. This postcard portrait of George V was published by E.A. Schwerdtfeger, but would rate as a fairly ordinary example.

higher price than you expect, but any mixed or bulk lots will probably sell for less than you'd like.

Another way of disposing of your collection or surplus cards is to sell **direct to a dealer.** If you've built up a good business relationship with some dealers over your years of collecting, you will know who best to offer your cards to. Any reputable postcard dealer should make a collector a fair offer for the cards. This should be between a half or two-thirds of his or her selling price for cards in good condition. The trade body for postcard dealers is the *Postcard Traders Association (PTA).*

Selling directly to dealers means you will receive immediate cash for the cards you want to sell; disposing of them through auction or selling via lists or by taking a table at fairs will generally mean a wait of two months or more between your decision to sell and your realising the cash for all your saleable cards.

You can, of course, **exchange** your cards with another collector or dealer if you want replacement cards rather than cash.

How much should you pay for picture postcards?

Unlike other collecting hobbies, such as stamps, coins and cigarette cards, there is no near-definitive list of picture postcards: although checklists exist for certain artists and publishers, collectors often have to rely on experience and advice. Reference to one of the established general catalogues (see page 28) is essential for the new collector, though, and a careful study of one or more will provide an excellent guide. Our summary here is only extremely general, but will at least give the reader a general idea of the price structures that might be met. Prices mentioned here and in catalogues are for postcards in very good condition (see page 9).

A large percentage of the postcards seen on sale at collectors' fairs and in shops will have been originally published from 1900-1930, and catalogue pricing structures are normally geared to this period. Later cards, with exceptions, will be cheaper, and reprints/reproductions certainly should be. The last five years have seen a new upsurge in the publication of picture postcards, and most of these should be available at their original retail price (15-30p) – but see section on moderns (pages 24-27).

Actresses – huge quantities exist of Edwardian actresses, and most should retail at 20-30p.

Advert cards – a wide variety, with many not really popular at the moment. Posters (cards reproducing what were originally poster adverts) are keenly collected, and priced from £10-£100. Shipping, railway, and tobacco posters particularly popular, but specialised knowledge is necessary here. Other adverts can cost from 25p to several pounds.

Animals – cats, dogs, horses and pigs are currently favourites, with artist-drawn and/or early (pre-1910) cards especially popular. £1-£4 for the best examples, but £12 + for the famous cat artist Louis Wain.

Art – plenty of art reproductions of famous paintings available at about 30p to make up your own miniature art gallery. Landscape artists feature in abundance on postcards, too, from 30p-£1. Current favourite is A.R. Quinton (75p + for pre-1930 cards, but progressively less for successive editions, down to 10p for 1980's issues). Art Deco/Nouveau are highly specialist fields. Cards can cost up to £100, and these areas are not recommended for the inexperienced beginner.

Aviation – best cards are pre-1914 pictures of aviators and meetings with related postmark and message (£6 upwards). Balloons (£4 upwards) are quite popular. Second World War planes are very common, and should only rate about £1.

Children – photographs and comic cards should be generally cheap (10-50p), though a few special artists will be more expensive, and nursery rhymes/teddy bears will add a premium (£1-£4).

Comic – a vast amount of material. Pre-1918 is best, but even here a card has to have a special theme (e.g. cricket, golf, chess) or artist (Phil May, Tom Browne, Donald McGill) to put it above the 50p mark. Certain comic subjects can go for several pounds, and reference to the catalogue listings is necessary.

Exhibitions/Pageants – lots of industrial exhibitions that incorporated entertainments, and historical pageants, surfaced in Britain 1900-39. From 30p to £1 for the majority of examples, though ones with related postmarks may be worth more.

Film Stars – masses of material available, most at 50p-£1. Some cult stars will sell for more. Better examples are those coloured (tinted) cards from the 1930's.

Glamour – photographic nudes will cost £1-£3, coloured art studies 75p-£25. Top price is for Raphael Kirchner, and his cards sometimes go even higher. Popular in U.S.A. and continental Europe.

Greetings – care is needed here. 1920's onwards deckle-edged cards are abundant and worth very little (5-10p). Indeed, most greetings cards after 1910 are not too collectable. The best are those with attractive chromo (see page 22) printing or incorporating collectable themes – Father Christmas, gnomes, rabbits, pigs etc. Good examples of these will go for £2 upwards. Continental 'Gruss Aus' (Greetings from) postcards were produced in large quantities from the 1880's, but often feature attractive designs. The best examples can cost as much as £4, the inferior designs 50p.

Heraldic – includes badges, city arms etc. Most series, including the famous 'Ja-Ja' town arms, at around £1. Oxford/Cambridge University college crests are common and rate considerably less.

Industry – postcards featuring work scenes fall into the 'Social History' (q.v.) category. Popular (and expensive) are coal-mines (£9 + for good photographic cards) and scenes showing people at work (usually several pounds). Inside views of the Royal Mint are an exception, though.

Military – a very popular (and wide) field, covering wars, regiments, and army life. Certain artists (Harry Payne £3 +) are collectable, and Gale and Polden/Raphael Tuck-published cards worth £2-£3.

Novelty – postcards were issued in all kinds of shapes and materials, but most of these oddballs are not very popular and usually priced at under £1. An exception is cut-outs, a specialist subject. Dolls cost £25 + , for example, in this medium.

Political – Edwardian England was a fertile ground for cartoonists, and many examples featured on cards. Prices of most range from 75p-£5. Pictures of politicians go from 50p (Joseph Chamberlain) to £1.50 + (Winston Churchill). Election souvenirs can cost £3 upwards. Nazi subjects, in demand in Germany, can be extremely expensive.

Postal – cards featuring post offices (up to £25 for the best animated photographic examples), postmen – including comic – and stamps are popular with philatelists too. Comic postmen rate £1-£2, embossed stamp cards £5.

Royalty – a very popular theme, and one which has seen continuous postcard production from 1880's. Plenty of material, though, and most British royalty should only cost about 75p-£1 a card. Commemoratives will be more expensive, and Eastern European royalty, especially Russian, is sought-after.

Silks – embroidered and woven. The former are mostly souvenirs of the Great War, and an exceptional number have survived because of their sentimental value. Hearts / flowers / greetings rate about £1, flags / patriotic £2-£4, and regimental crests £6 + . Woven silks often feature ships or personalities, and go for £20-£40, with a few more expensive exceptions.

Social History – a vast field that covers anything featuring people and work. Reference to a catalogue is really necessary to see the scope of this theme.

Song Cards – produced in huge quantities, usually by James Bamforth of Huddersfield, and often in 3 or 4 card sets. Most featured popular songs/hymns of the 1900-18 period, incorporating a posed picture and a verse. With a few exceptions, a 3-card set should cost £1.50, a 4-card set £2.

Street scenes (topographical) – City and town centres are usually common and cards should probably only rate 50p-£1.50 (less for London). Suburban streets and village scenes can cost up to £12 depending on rarity, amount of animation, and clarity of photo (see glossary, real photographic, page 22). Because of their importance for local historians, these cards are doubly sought-after.

Sport – an increasingly popular category. Football, Cricket, Golf and Tennis are especially rated, and both serious and comic cards are collected. The latter cost around £2-4 in all four sports; as further examples, professional football teams on cards might sell for £6, county cricket teams for £5.

Transport – because this century has seen much change in modes and designs of transportation, pre-1920 cards are particularly popular. **Railways** are perhaps the most collected of all subjects on postcards, and railway cards have certainly been well-researched. Engines will cost 50p-£1.50, while stations go from 50p (for exteriors of large city stations) to £20 or more for interiors of town or village stations. Cards issued by railway companies, particularly the smaller ones, vary wildly in price – from 75p for common London & North Western Company cards to £60 + for poster adverts. **Motoring** – around £2 for comic cards, £3-4 for photographic cars, and a little more for race meetings. **Shipping** – plenty of merchant liners around; ordinary coloured cards for about £1, company advert cards for £5 upwards. **Trams** – real photographic close-ups / accidents / opening ceremonies can cost about £20; trams in street scenes rate 50p-£20 according to the guidelines for topographical cards.

Views (topographicals). Countryside/rural views from any decade this century are unlikely to find much favour, partly because the cards are common, partly because the views may not have changed much (compare the changes in urban streets). If at all saleable, most views of places like the Lake District and similar scenic tourist locations, will rate only 5-20p, unless by a special artist or publisher.

Note: This is only the briefest of summaries; the new collector should refer to a catalogue for more detailed information.

Finding out more

This booklet may not have answered all your questions you want answered about postcard collecting, but we hope it helps you enjoy your hobby. We are always willing to help collectors with any queries about postcards, either by return letter, or via *Picture Postcard Monthly.* You can write to us at the address on the back cover, but please remember to include a S.A.E.

GLOSSARY OF POSTCARD TERMS

A selection of words or phrases you might come across in your postcard reading.

Art Nouveau – an artistic style characterised by flowing lines and flowery symbols. Most often found on postcards in the turn-of-the-century period: typical artists are Raphael Kirchner, Alphonse Mucha and Elisabeth Sonrel.

Art Deco – 1920's artistic style recognisable by symmetrical designs and straight lines. Typical artists are Mela Koehler and C.E. Shand.

Bipex – abbreviation of British International Postcard Exhibition, established in 1976 as the country's postcard showpiece. Now held at the prestigious Kensington Town Hall each autumn. Provincial Bipex events have also been held at York and Harrogate.

Cartology – name used in Great Britain to define the activity of collecting picture postcards.

Catch-phrases – many comic postcards of the pre-1914 era are captioned by phrases such as *'My word, if I catch you bending'*, or *'When father says turn'*. Artists used considerable ingenuity in fitting different interpretations to the phrase.

Chromo-Lithograph (sometimes called simply 'chromo') – a beautiful example of early colour printing, recognised by the individual colours on a postcard standing out clearly by themselves when the card is held at a particular angle. German printers developed the techniques best, with *Meissner and Buch* a particularly outstanding example in this respect.

Composite – a group of cards that combine to make one large picture or design. Each card has a recognisable picture of its own as well as part of the larger design e.g. battle scene/Napoleon's left leg. Composite sets may consist of various numbers of cards from two upwards. Well-known ones are Napoleon, Jesus Christ, and Edward VII (Horniman's Tea). Animals such as pigs were also favoured with this technique.

Court Cards – the official size for British picture postcards between 1895 and 1899, measuring 115 x 89mm. Some superb chromolithographs can be found on this type.

Deltiology – American term for the hobby of collecting postcards.

Divided back – a reference to the non-picture side of the postcard, which in January 1902 was allowed by the Post Office in Great Britain to have a dividing line to accommodate address (right) and message (left). Prior to this, only the address had been permitted on cards: this style was known as **undivided back**.

Embossed – postcard where the surface is raised by means of an indentation on the reverse, making the picture stand out.

Giant Postcards – extremely large ones! Not favoured by collectors because of the difficulty of displaying and storing them. Some could be as large as 305 x 165mm.

Intermediate Cards – of size 130mm x 80mm, 'in between' court and standard size. Productions of the 1898-1902 period, usually of rather drab subject matter.

Hold-to-light – a postcard which, when held to a bright light, produces an illumination effect (provided by one layer of the card being cut out) or the apparition of a new picture. In this latter case, the cards were produced with fewer layers of card in order to produce a 'see-through' effect.

Midget postcards – extremely small ones, size 90mm x 70mm. Actresses and Royalty were favourite subjects for these.

Novelty cards – embrace a whole series of postcards, from those made out of unusual materials (wood, leather, peat, aluminium) to curious shapes and sizes, and cards which did unusual things (rotate, squeak, press out into dolls). Applied to any postcards not of the normal size, shape or appearance.

Oilette – word coined by publishers Raphael Tuck & Sons to describe postcards which were in effect miniature oil paintings. The term was used to describe thousands of sets produced by the company.

Pull-outs – postcards which incorporate a flap, beneath which is housed a strip of photos that can be pulled out. Sometimes called 'concertinas'. In the novelty class.

Real photographic – used with topographical cards to describe a picture that has been produced by a photographic rather than printing process. Preferred by collectors because of their superior clarity and glossy finish.

Set – a number of cards grouped together by a publisher to form a designated series. Can be found in multiples from two to over a hundred, but the most common number is six.

Standard size – introduced in G.B. in November 1899, though had been used on the Continent for many years. Measured 140 x 89mm and remained the standard size for postcards until the 1970's.

Topographical – applied to postcards that show scenic views and street scenes, where the general view is more prominent than a particular subject. If the latter, e.g. tram or post office is most prominent, then the card becomes categorised by that name, and is known as topographical-related. Sometimes abbreviated to 'topo'.

Undivided back – see **divided back**.

Vignette – small picture occupying only a small part of the space of the picture side of a postcard. May be on its own or with other vignettes. Style popularised on the Continent in the 1880's with Gruss Aus (Greetings from) cards.

Details of specialist and collectors' fairs where you can buy and sell postcards are published in *Picture Postcard Monthly* (see advert on back cover).

*A very early card in 'Gruss Aus' style, but in an
unusual format – a little smaller than Court size.*

*David Allen & Sons specialis-
ed in publishing postcards
advertising theatrical productions. At least they were
self-explanatory! Many were
designed by top artists like
Hassall, Barribal and
Kinsella.*

*Political comment was a favourite source of
amusement. The Insurance Act of 1911 provoked
many cartoons like this, satirising employers who
made servants stick on their own stamps. Barnet-
by postmark on this one, in September 1916, in
Inter-Art's 'Licker' series.*

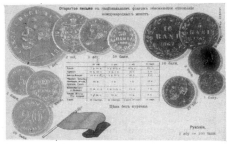

*Embossed coin cards – expensive in 1975, more
reasonable now.*

23

Collecting Modern Cards

In the last few years, collectors in Britain have begun to collect contemporary cards in huge numbers, following a trend established in France in the early 1970's. What is in effect happening is a revival of the pre-1914 craze for collecting postcards, though the fashion for sending them in huge numbers has not yet been rekindled. So when hobbyists of the mid-21st century discover 1980's postcard collections, they may well find most of them postally unused.

This revival has been encouraged by a mushrooming of superb postcard designs, on sale in High Street shops all over the country and – in the case of limited edition cards – through the specialist postcard hobby retail outlets.

Cards published today are a mixture of modern designs and nostalgic images – posters, film stars, transport scenes – going back anything from twenty to a hundred years, and sometimes overlapping the 'Golden Age' (see page 2). While these nostalgic cards are fine when reproduced from other media, I wouldn't encourage anyone to collect items which are simply reprints of older cards.

To a certain extent, people who buy postcards today are looking for the same subjects as their Edwardian predecessors: royalty, personalities (though today it's pop, in 1905 it was music hall), artistic cards, transport, special events, comic and so on. Street scenes and view-cards are not highly regarded by today's buyers as collec-

M.A. Arts began publishing cards in the late 1980's, and so far have over a hundred different titles, all on transport themes, all from original paintings.

David Skipp's painting of Ilfracombe harbour, one of a long series of his postcard designs published by Town & Country Prints.

The cards of French fantasy artist André Martins de Barros have acquired a huge following in the last few years, and prices of his early cards have soared to several pounds. Big rises like this are, though, the exception in modern postcard collecting at the moment.

table items, though the general public of course buy them in huge quantities; but neither were they rated by Edwardians, who preferred to collect subjects in their albums.

One brand new collecting fashion concerns postcards issued as a part of the hobby itself – as souvenirs of fairs, as personal advertising, or as club promotions. France, Britain and the U.S.A. are the chief sources of cards like this, and the collecting of them has become truly international.

Leading firms who have published cards encouraging the growth of postcard sales in the High Street include Athena (art and contemporary design), Nugeron (film posters), Reflex Marketing (pop), and Chapter & Verse (scenic). There are, though, literally hundreds of superb publishers whose postcards can be picked up at basic prices, and the standard of production and quality of design rivals the 'Golden Age'. Among publishers who produce cards in smaller quantities aimed more specifically at the collectors' market are J/V Postcards (special events), M.A. Arts (transport), Enterprise Postcards (royalty), and Leeds Postcards (political and social comment). Additionally, many localities are now serviced by publishers who are producing excellent topographical cards.

It's fascinating to speculate which of the postcards being published today will be most popular and collectable in fifty years time. It's hard to make comparisons with the Edwardian cards that are currently most in demand, but in that case topographicals, art nouveau, transport, special events, and poster advertising are all well up on many collec-

1980's social history: buskers at Southend-on-Sea. Card published by Lynn Tait Gallery.

York artist-drawn viewcard, painted and published by David Cuppleditch.

Cartoon card by Jean Claval to celebrate the 100th anniversary of the Eiffel Tower.

Unusual pop music card, one of a series painted by Jose Correa and published by Editions Dalix.

tors' shopping lists. It is tempting to consider that images of the 1980's – Margaret Thatcher, the Falklands war, the miner's strike, nuclear weapons, green issues, and the social history of the decade – will before too long be immensely collectable. But whatever you go for, the massive range of contemporary cards currently available give an excellent and varied selection of subjects or artists from which to put together a collection.

One of the problems of defining 'modern cards' is what time limit to set. Cards published in the last five years? Last decade? Since World War 2? From 1940? Arguments have been advanced for all these, and debate will no doubt rage unabated. Many collectors even doubt the wisdom of making any divisions at all.

However, for the purposes of the magazine Collect Modern Postcards, the decision was made to classify post-1950 issues as 'modern'. Doubtless this will have to be reviewed periodically.

Birmingham International Airport on a multi-view published by J/V Postcards.

Barrie Law's gypsy cards provide a superb example of contemporary social history. *

The hurricane of 1987 stimulated quite a number of postcards, most of which sold out very quickly.

Londonderry street scene by Deirdre Sprott.

Balloons at Basingstoke, on a card published by PH Topics.